First Facts®

The Solar System

Mars

by Adele Richardson

Consultant:
Stephen J. Kortenkamp, PhD
Research Scientist
Planetary Science Institute, Tucson, Arizona

Capstone
press®

Mankato, Minnesota

First Facts is published by Capstone Press,
151 Good Counsel Drive, P.O. Box 669, Mankato, Minnesota 56002.
www.capstonepress.com

Library of Congress Cataloging-in-Publication Data
Richardson, Adele, 1966–
    Mars / by Adele Richardson.—Rev. and updated.
    p. cm.—(First facts. The Solar system)
    Includes bibliographical references and index.
    ISBN-13: 978-1-4296-0723-0 (hardcover)
    ISBN-10: 1-4296-0723-8 (hardcover)
    1. Mars (Planet)—Juvenile literature. I. Title. II. Series.
QB641.R357 2008
523.43—dc22   2007003529

Summary: Discusses the orbit, atmosphere, surface features, and exploration of the
    planet Mars.

Editorial Credits
Christopher Harbo, editor; Juliette Peters, designer and illustrator; Jo Miller, photo researcher;
    Scott Thoms, photo editor

Photo Credits
Astronomical Society of the Pacific/NASA, 15
Corbis/NASA/Roger Ressmeyer, 8
NASA/JPL, 14; JPL/Cornell, 9; JPL-Caltech/Cornell, 17 (Composite image of *Spirit* on Mars)
Photodisc, cover, 1, 4, planet images within illustrations and chart, 7, 11, 13, 19, 21
Photo Researchers Inc./Science Photo Library/John Sanford, 16
Space Images/NASA/JPL, 10
U.S. Geological Survey, Flagstaff, 5, 20

1 2 3 4 5 6 12 11 10 09 08 07

Table of Contents

Viking 1 Visits Mars

In 1976, *Viking 1* arrived at Mars. The spacecraft took many pictures as it circled the planet. Scientists were able to see many of Mars' volcanoes and large canyons. Some pictures showed Olympus Mons. This huge volcano is the largest in the solar system.

Fast Facts about Mars

Diameter: 4,222 miles (6,795 kilometers)
Average Distance from Sun: 142 million miles (228 million kilometers)
Average Temperature (surface): minus 81 degrees Fahrenheit (minus 63 degrees Celsius)
Length of Day: 24 hours, 37 minutes
Length of Year: 687 Earth days
Moons: 2

Olympus Mons

The Solar System

Mars is the fourth planet from the Sun. Mercury, Venus, and Earth are closer to the Sun. All four planets are made mostly of rock. Jupiter, Saturn, Uranus, and Neptune are the next farthest planets. They are made of gas and ice.

Fun Fact!
In July 1997, the *Sojourner* rover explored Mars. This robot was the first moving vehicle to land on another planet.

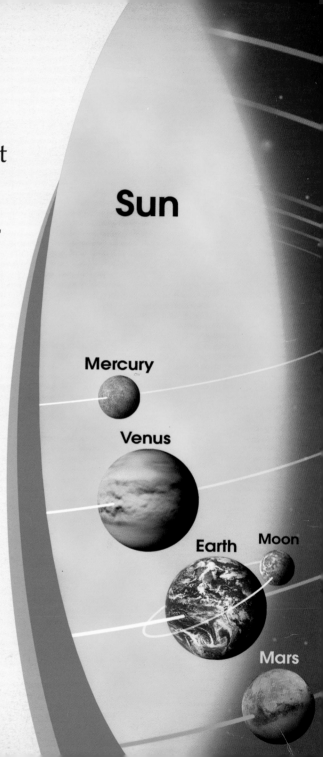

Sun

Mercury

Venus

Earth

Moon

Mars

Jupiter

Saturn

Uranus

Neptune

7

Mars' Atmosphere

The gases surrounding a planet are called its **atmosphere**. Mars has a thin atmosphere. It is made mostly of **carbon dioxide** gas.

Strong winds blow red dust into Mars' atmosphere. The dust gives the sky a tan color.

Mars' Makeup

Mars' surface, or crust, is made of rock and dirt. Iron in the dirt gives the planet its rusty red color. Mars has flat areas, mountains, canyons, and volcanoes.

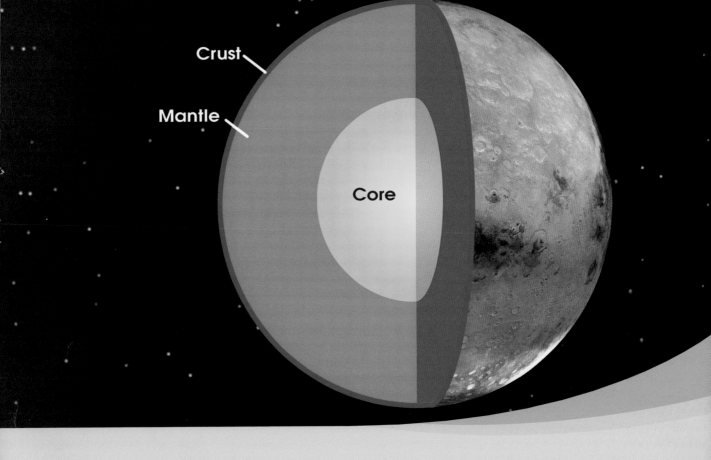

Crust

Mantle

Core

Mars has a **mantle** and **core** below
the crust. The mantle is made of rock.
Scientists believe the core is solid iron.

How Mars Moves

Mars spins on its **axis** as it circles the Sun. The planet spins almost as fast as Earth. Mars takes 24 hours and 37 minutes to spin on its axis once. Mars circles the Sun more slowly than Earth does. The planet takes 687 Earth days to travel around the Sun once.

Fun Fact!
Mars has spring, summer, autumn, and winter seasons. On Mars, seasons last about six Earth months.

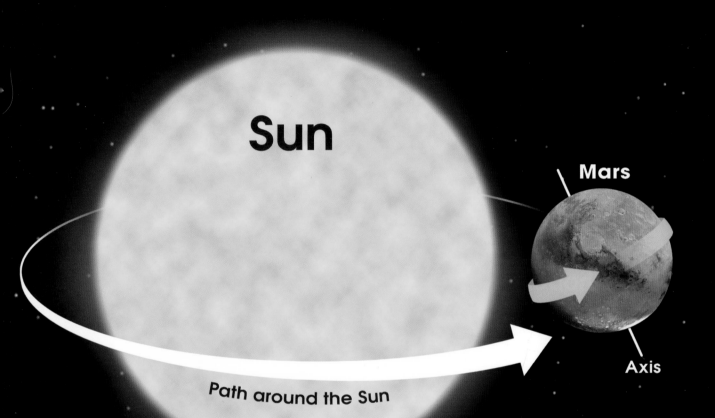

Sun

Mars

Axis

Path around the Sun

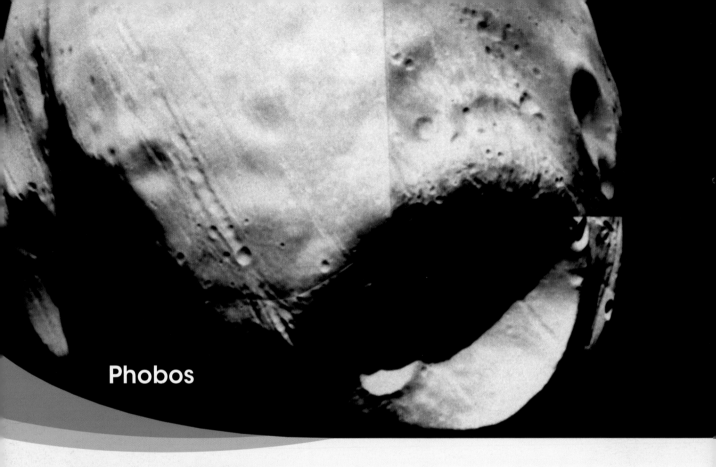

Phobos

Mars' Moons

Mars has two small moons that circle
the planet. They are Phobos and Deimos.
Phobos is the larger moon. It is only
about 17 miles (27 kilometers) wide.

Phobos and Deimos look lumpy. Some people think they look like potatoes. Both moons have many craters and are covered with dust.

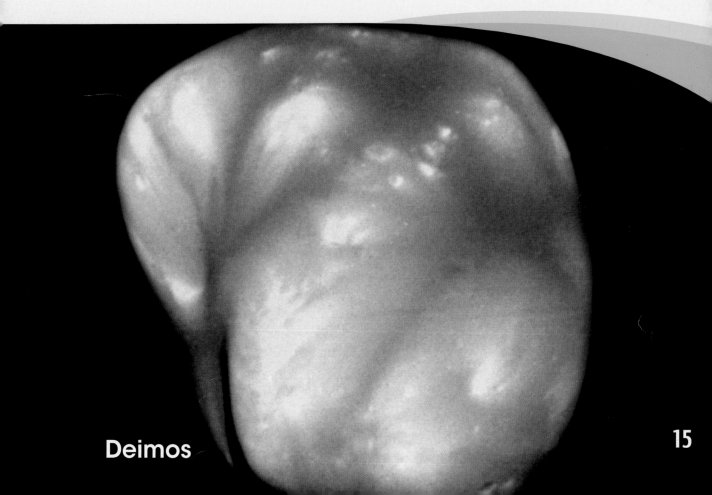

Deimos

Studying Mars

Mars is easy to see from Earth. It looks like a reddish star in the night sky. People use **telescopes** to look at the planet more closely.

Mars

Scientists learn about Mars by sending spacecraft to the planet. In 2004, two robots explored Mars. They were named *Spirit* and *Opportunity*.

Comparing Mars to Earth

Mars and Earth are both rocky planets. But the planets are very different. People could not breathe in Mars' atmosphere. The planet's temperatures are much colder than Earth's temperatures. People would have to wear space suits to breathe and stay warm on Mars.

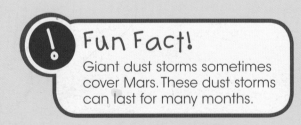

Fun Fact!
Giant dust storms sometimes cover Mars. These dust storms can last for many months.

Size Comparison

Earth

Mars

Amazing but True!

Mars has the largest known canyon in the solar system. Valles Marineris is about 2,485 miles (4,000 kilometers) long. On Earth, it would stretch all the way across the United States. Scientists believe flowing water shaped parts of the canyon long ago.

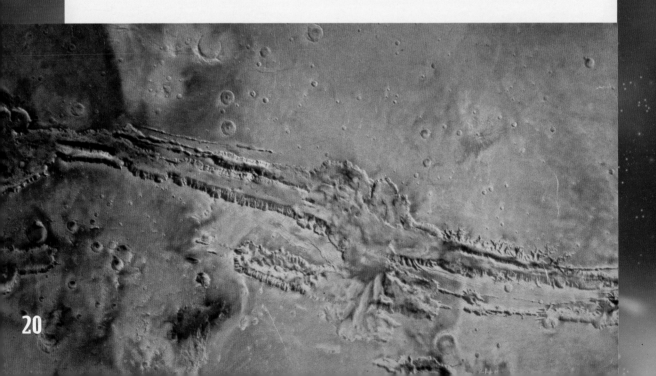

Planet Comparison Chart

Planet	Size Rank (1=largest)	Makeup	1 Trip around the Sun (Earth Time)
Mercury	8	rock	88 days
Venus	6	rock	225 days
Earth	5	rock	365 days, 6 hours
Mars	7	rock	687 days
Jupiter	1	gases and ice	11 years, 11 months
Saturn	2	gases and ice	29 years, 6 months
Uranus	3	gases and ice	84 years
Neptune	4	gases and ice	164 years, 10 months

Glossary

atmosphere (AT-muhss-feehr)—the layer of gases that surrounds some planets and moons

axis (AK-siss)—an imaginary line that runs through the middle of a planet; a planet spins on its axis.

carbon dioxide (KAR-buhn dye-OK-side)— a gas that has no smell or color

core (KOR)—the inner part of a planet that is made of metal or rock

mantle (MAN-tuhl)—the part of a planet between the crust and the core

telescope (TEL-uh-skope)—an instrument that makes faraway objects appear larger and closer

Read More

Chrismer, Melanie. *Mars.* Scholastic News Nonfiction Readers. New York: Children's Press, 2007.

Jefferis, David. *Exploring Planet Mars.* Humans in Space. New York: Crabtree, 2007.

Kortenkamp, Steve. *Why Isn't Pluto a Planet?: A Book about Planets.* First Facts: Why in the World? Mankato, Minn.: Capstone Press, 2007.

Internet Sites

FactHound offers a safe, fun way to find Internet sites related to this book. All of the sites on FactHound have been researched by our staff.

Here's how:
1. Visit *www.facthound.com*
2. Choose your grade level.
3. Type in this book ID **1429607238** for age-appropriate sites. You may also browse subjects by clicking on letters, or by clicking on pictures and words.
4. Click on the **Fetch It** button.

FactHound will fetch the best sites for you!

Index